A ... NTARY REVIE... ...

A CRE...

MOZ.

BY

ILLUS...

... most famo... ...rks

GARRARD PUBLISHING COMPANY

MOZART
Music Magician

MOZART
Music Magician

by Claire Huchet Bishop

illustrated by Paul Frame

GARRARD PUBLISHING COMPANY
Champaign, Illinois

To Elizabeth Minot Graves

with gratitude

for many years of stimulating collaboration

and abiding friendship

927.8

M

Acknowledgments:

Reprinted by permission of C. F. Peters Corporation, Sole Agents of Eulenburg Pocket Scores, 373 Park Avenue South, New York, N.Y.:

> *Violin Concerto in A Major*, p. 71; *The Marriage of Figaro*, p. 106; *Symphony in G Minor No. 40*, p. 117; *Piano Concerto in B Flat Major*, p. 123; *Concerto for Clarinet in A Major*, p. 130

Reprinted by permission of Theodore Presser Company, (Universal Edition), Presser Place, Bryn Mawr, Pa.:

> *Bastien and Bastienne*, p. 57

Reprinted by permission of G. Schirmer, Inc., 609 Fifth Avenue, N.Y.:

> *Minuet No. 1, with Trio*, p. 14; *Piano Sonata in A Major*, p. 79; "Ach, ich fühl's" from *The Magic Flute*, p. 129

Reprinted by permission of Associate Music Publishers, 609 Fifth Avenue, N.Y.:

> *Eine Kleine Nachtmüsik*, p. 108; "Der Vogelfäuger bin ich ja" from *The Magic Flute*, p. 131

Photo Credits:

Austrian Information Service: pp. 1, 8, 25, 39, 63, 72, 74, 84, 95, 97, 104, 112, 132, 134

Austrian National Library Photo Archives: p. 102

Austrian State Tourist Department: pp. 9, 20, 90

The Bettmann Archive: pp. 11, 24, 45, 55, 75, 76, 101, 131

Culver Pictures: pp. 2, 16, 27, 28, 32, 38, 40, 98, 103, 109, 127

Historical Pictures Service—Chicago: pp. 53, 78, 125

International Stiftung Mozarteum, Salzburg: pp. 10, 23, 36, 52

Copyright © 1968 by Claire Huchet Bishop

Library of Congress Catalog Card Number: 67-16856

Contents

1. Baby Brother

"Nannerl, you have a baby brother."

Four-and-a-half-year-old Nannerl looked up at Papa as he closed the bedroom door behind him. Papa carried a blanket-wrapped bundle.

"Let me see! Let me see! Please, Papa!" Nannerl begged.

Papa bent and uncovered a corner of the blanket.

"Oh!" whispered Nannerl looking at the tiny, wrinkled face. "And what is his name?"

"Johannes Chrysostomus Wolfgang Gottlieb Mozart."

"What a long name! I'll call him Wolfgang, or 'Wolferl' or just 'Wolf.'"

That day, January 27, 1756, was a cold day in Salzburg. The town lay in that part of Europe now called Austria. There was always a lot of snow in winter. But the Mozart apartment was snug and warm. It was on the third floor of an old stone building, on a busy square.

Nannerl found it was great fun to have a baby

An old engraving shows Salzburg as it was during Mozart's lifetime.

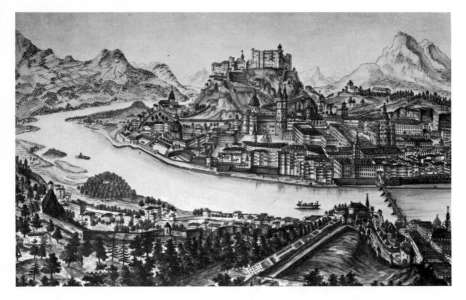

The house in Salzburg where Mozart was born is now a museum in his memory.

brother. Soon, however, she could not spend all her time with him. Papa was teaching her to play the clavier. This was a keyboard instrument somewhat like a piano, which was popular 200 years ago.

Mr. Mozart was a violinist at the court of the Prince-Archbishop, the ruler of Salzburg. Leopold Mozart played in the court orchestra. He also taught the choir boys to play the violin.

Anna Marie Mozart, by an unknown artist.

He wanted his children to be professional musicians too.

There was always music in the Mozarts' apartment. Papa played the violin, Nannerl practiced the clavier, and Mama sang gay songs.

Mama was young and full of fun. She was devoted to her children and to Papa. Papa ruled the household. He supervised everything, not only the music lessons, but also the cooking. He decided what was to be eaten at every meal.

As soon as Wolfgang could walk he liked to sit on the floor near Nannerl while she practiced the clavier. "One, two, three, four," Mr. Mozart counted aloud as Nannerl's fingers ran over the keyboard.

One day after the lesson, Nannerl and Papa

Leopold Mozart as painted by Zoffany.

went out for a walk. Mama was busy in the kitchen. Quietly, three-year-old Wolfgang got up and climbed on Nannerl's chair. It was too low for him. His little arms could not reach the keyboard. He climbed down, looked around and saw some cushions. He carried one back to the chair and climbed up again.

It was perfect. Softly he pressed the keys down with his chubby fingers, first this key and this one together, then another and another together. Again and again he tried pressing two different keys. Suddenly he stopped. What a lovely sound! He pressed the same two keys again and heard the same pleasing sound. How happy he was! He began hunting all over the keyboard for two other keys which would make the same lovely sound together.

Mama rushed in from the kitchen. Papa and Nannerl, who had just come home, crowded near the clavier.

"Papa!" cried Nannerl hugging her baby brother, "Papa! he is only three and he has discovered the thirds all by himself!"

Now Wolfgang wanted lessons. "Just like Nannerl," he said. He admired his sister very much. So his father began to teach him. Papa was very strict. He did not allow any nonsense. Wolfgang had to practice every day. He loved it. Soon he began making up little tunes. He improvised all the time, humming and singing and dancing to his own tunes.

Wolfgang loved dancing and so did the whole family. It was a gay home though everyone worked hard. When Wolfgang was five, he made up the music for a dance called a minuet. This music is still played today. Here is the beginning of the *Minuet in G:*

From that time on Wolfgang composed many small pieces. He played them for his father who wrote them down on paper.

One day Wolfgang tried writing down the notes himself. Mr. Mozart found him covered with ink, sitting at a table. Wolfgang had been dipping his pen too deeply in the ink bottle. The ink had dripped all over the paper. He had wiped the spots with his hand, then wiped his hand on his face and his blond hair.

"Mercy me!" Papa cried, "What are you doing?"

"I am writing a concerto, Papa."

Wolfgang and Nannerl often played duets on the
clavier even at this early age.

"Really!" said Papa. He could not keep from laughing as he took the paper. He looked at it and what did he see? There was indeed the beginning of a real concerto. In a concerto one instrument is heard by itself against an accompaniment by a whole orchestra.

"My goodness! This is a difficult piece, young man."

"Of course! Let me show you!"

Five-year-old Wolfgang ran to the clavier. But his hands were too small to reach the chords he had written down. "Why aren't one's fingers big enough right away?" he wailed. "Maybe a violin would be easier. Please Papa, buy me a violin for my birthday. Please! One just like Uncle Johann's."

What a joy when the violin came! Wolfgang tried to play it. He practiced and practiced. When Uncle Johann came, Wolfgang was very proud. "See, Uncle Johann, I have a violin too. We can play together."

"So we can, when you know how." Uncle Johann took his violin from its case.

"Are you ready, Johann?" called Mr. Mozart from the next room.

"Coming," said Uncle Johann. He and Wolfgang's father, and a friend, were going to play a trio together. Wolfgang picked up his small fiddle and followed his uncle.

"Run away, Wolferl. This is not for you. Don't disturb us," said Papa.

"Oh, please, Papa! I won't disturb you. I'll be very, very good," begged Wolfgang in tears.

"Leopold, let him sit by me. Just once," said Uncle Johann.

"All right. But not a word from you, Wolfgang."

The three men began to play. Uncle Johann was playing the second violin. Soon he heard the sound of Wolfgang's small fiddle next to him. Gradually, Uncle Johann stopped playing while Wolfgang went right on.

It was Mr. Mozart's turn to have eyes filled with tears! The trio ended, and the three men applauded Wolfgang who said, "Oh, it's easy to play the second violin. One does not have to learn!"

Whenever he was not busy with his music, Wolfgang loved to play outdoors with the other boys. He did not go to school. His father taught him everything. Wolfgang liked arithmetic especially.

Best of all, of course, he loved the clavier and the violin. He never grew tired of music. Mama had to scold him because he did not eat at mealtime. He was too busy humming and moving

his fingers on the table. At bedtime, Papa had to pull him away from the keyboard.

Papa would sit in his armchair and Wolfgang would climb into his lap. "Papa," he said "when you are old I will keep you always near me, in a little glass box so that the dust will not fall on you." Quickly he kissed the tip of Papa's nose and at last was off to bed.

Mozart's clavier is preserved in the Mozart Museum which was once his home. The painting on the wall, showing Mozart holding a bird's nest, is thought to have been done by Zoffany.

2. On the Road

Friends often came to visit the Mozart family. Then Papa would say, "Now then, Nannerl and Wolfgang, you are going to play for us." And they did. Soon friends brought other friends. People marvelled. "These are wonder children!" everybody said.

Papa was proud of Nannerl and Wolfgang. He wanted them to play in bigger cities than Salzburg. He wanted them to be heard by princes and kings. In those days noblemen paid musicians to perform and to compose. Every musician had to find a rich patron. That was the only way to make a living and to become known.

When Wolfgang was six, Papa said, "Mama, get everything ready. We are going to Vienna."

"To Vienna! What for?"

"I want Nannerl and Wolfgang to play for the Empress Maria Teresa."

Nannerl and Wolfgang were thrilled. The journey took several days by coach. After they arrived in Vienna, they had to wait for an appointment to appear at court. Finally the great day came. Nannerl and Wolfgang could hardly wait.

They were specially dressed for the grand occasion. At that time it was the fashion for children to wear the same kind of clothes as adults. Wolfgang loved his lilac suit and waistcoat all embroidered with gold. Nannerl looked lovely in her long billowing white brocade skirt.

"Papa," asked Wolfgang, "Does the Empress like music? Really and truly?"

"Indeed she does. The Empress herself plays and her children do too. Ah, here is the royal carriage. Come, children!"

Vienna in Mozart's time was a popular center of music. The city overlooks the Danube River.

What a carriage! Outside it was all gold, inside all red velvet. On a step between the rear wheels stood a footman dressed in a fancy uniform. Wolfgang was delighted. Nannerl was a little fearful.

They were even more excited when they reached the royal palace. The children followed the footman through one huge room after another. Papa carried Wolfgang's violin. Nobody said a word.

At last the footman opened a door to the music room. There was the Empress, sitting in an armchair, surrounded by her family and the ladies and gentlemen of the court.

Nannerl made her finest curtsy. Little Wolfgang kissed the Empress's hand. The Empress bent to greet him. Suddenly, Wolfgang jumped into her lap, put his arms around her neck and

A street scene in old Vienna. The city today still contains many of these beautiful buildings.

gave her a resounding kiss. Papa was horrified. But the Empress laughed and all the court people did too.

First, Wolfgang and Nannerl played together. Then Nannerl played alone. Then it was Wolfgang's turn to play by himself. Silence fell over the room. The ladies and gentlemen of the court could not believe their eyes and ears. There sat a six-year-old, his fingers barely reaching the keyboard, his feet dangling from the seat. Yet he played like a skilled adult musician. He

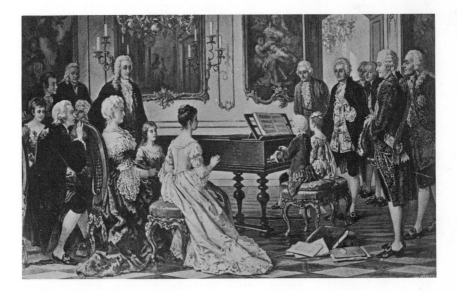

This statue of Wolfgang tuning his violin was done by E. Barrias.

made the loveliest sounds come out of the clavier. People were spellbound.

Then Mr. Mozart handed Wolfgang a violin. The boy played it easily and beautifully.

"Unbelievable!" the ladies and gentlemen said to each other.

"How can he do it?"

"I have never seen such a feat before!"

"He is a prodigy!"

"Yes, and what is so nice about him is that he is so friendly and natural. He is not a bit conceited."

The Empress was delighted by both children, and gave them various presents. Mr. Mozart received a sum of money. The Empress invited the Mozarts to the palace again and again. She asked Mr. Mozart to give the princesses music lessons. Wolfgang and Nannerl played in the park with the royal children.

When it rained, the palace was a wonderful place for hide and seek. But the polished floors were very slippery. One day Wolfgang lost his balance and fell down. The little Princess Marie Antoinette ran to him. She helped him up and straightened his rumpled suit.

"You are a good girl. When I grow up I shall marry you," Wolfgang declared.

One day, Wolfgang watched Papa give one of the princesses a lesson. The Emperor came in. "Mr. Mozart," he asked, "could your son play without looking at the keyboard?"

"Why not?" said Wolfgang ahead of Papa.

A cloth was spread on the keyboard. The little boy slid his hands under it and began to play.

"You are a real magician!" the Emperor said.

When the Mozarts returned to Salzburg, everybody wanted to hear about Vienna and the royal palace. The people of Salzburg were proud of the Mozart children.

Wolfgang could not wait to get back to his

studies. He wanted to learn more and more. He worked hard at the clavier and the violin.

After a few months Papa announced, "We are going to travel again. This time we will play in many cities. It will be a real concert tour, all the way to...."

"Where?" the children cried.

"Paris," Papa said.

3. Castles and Queens

They left by coach on June 9, 1763. The roads were muddy and had deep ruts. The coach swayed right and left. All of a sudden there was a snapping noise, and everybody was thrown against each other. A wheel was broken. The passengers had to wait in a small town while the wheel was repaired.

The Mozarts walked around the town. They went to a church.

"Papa," said Wolfgang, "I would like to play the organ."

"You do not know how. Anyway your legs are too small. But if you wish I will show you the organ. That will pass the time."

They all went into the church. Mr. Mozart explained how the organ works. The music comes from long pipes when the air is blown into them. There are two keyboards for the hands, and pedals on the floor for the feet to play too.

"Papa, please let me try it," cried Wolfgang.

"Leopold," said Mama, "I can work the blowers."

"And I will help Mama," announced twelve-year-old Nannerl.

"Good!" cried Wolfgang. Quickly he sat on the bench. But he could not reach the pedals. He pushed the bench away and began skipping from one pedal to the other.

The sexton heard the music and rushed up to the organ loft. He took one look at Wolfgang and threw up his arms. He ran downstairs and outside shouting, "It's a child! Come and see! A small boy. And he is making up the music!"

People filled the church. They would have liked to listen to Wolfgang over and over again. But it was time for the Mozarts to go back to the coach. The wheel had been fixed and the journey went on.

Papa was a good business manager. He had planned the trip carefully. When they arrived

This unsigned portrait of Nannerl now hangs in the Mozart Museum in Salzburg.

in a town, he often wrote announcements for the newspapers. One read partly as follows:

"The little girl who is twelve years old will play the most difficult works of the great masters. The boy who is not yet seven, will play a concerto on the violin. Not only will he accompany the orchestra on the clavier, but also will cover up the keyboard and play with as much ease as if he could see the keys. Also he will name by ear all the notes played singly or in chords, by someone else, either on the clavier, the violin or any other instrument, including bells, glasses or clocks. Finally he will play on the organ and improvise in all keys even the most difficult as the public would request and for as long as desired."

This was good advertising and every word of it was true.

The Mozarts took a boat down the Rhine River. The children played in many royal palaces

The Mozarts visited the magnificent palace at
Versailles by invitation of the king.

Mozart wrote this composition when he was only
six years old.

along the way. Mr. Mozart had hoped to make
some money since the long trip was very expensive. Unfortunately, they were given small
presents instead. Among them were little swords
for Wolfgang and ribbons and lace for Nannerl.
Papa wrote to a friend. "We have so many snuff
boxes and other novelties that we could soon
open a store."

On November 18, they arrived in Paris, the
capital of France. They were invited to visit
the King, Louis XV, in his palace at Versailles.

Among the famous people Mozart met in Paris was
Madame Pompadour.

They were overwhelmed by the splendor of the
palace. It was bigger than any they had ever
seen. The reception hall had a wall of mirrors
239 feet long. Sparkling chandeliers lit the room
brilliantly. The court ladies and men were
dressed in silks, laces, velvets, and brocades.

They were invited to a New Year's Eve dinner.
This did not mean they would eat with the King
and Queen. They would stand behind their
chairs. This was considered a great honor.

Wolfgang stood right behind the Queen. He
wore a fur-lined suit and had a little sword at

his side. The Queen turned her head and looked at him. "Isn't he sweet!" she cried. "Now, let me see. What would you like?" And she fed him tidbits from the table.

Nannerl and Wolfgang played for the King and the Queen several times. Everyone was amazed. The King gave Mr. Mozart a handsome sum of money.

The family went back to Paris in high spirits. They were invited to many noblemen's homes. There were more concerts and more successes.

Wolfgang was very busy, but he followed Papa's schedule and worked every morning. He composed four *Sonatas for Clavier with Violin Accompaniment.* Mr. Mozart had his son's sonatas printed.

Nannerl teased Wolfgang. "Wolferl, how does it feel to have your music printed? And to have everybody reading it and playing it? I bet you are going to swell all over with pride!"

"Silly!" replied Wolfgang, laughing heartily. He was glad of his success, but he was not at all conceited. He knew he still had much to learn.

4. Operas and Symphonies

After five months in France, the Mozarts sailed for England. Wolfgang played the violin for the ship's crew. The sailors' pet monkey listened. Next day the monkey got hold of a small board. He put it under his chin and went about scraping his makeshift violin with a long thin piece of wood. Nannerl and Wolfgang had a good laugh.

In London the Mozarts were invited to the royal palace. The King of England was George III, the same king the Americans fought later in the American Revolution. The King and the Queen liked music.

When Wolfgang met the Queen they spoke in German, as she was German by birth. But the King told Wolfgang, "Young man, next time you come you must know how to speak English."

At the next audience, the King said to Wolfgang, "How are you, little man?"

"Very well, thank you, Your Majesty," replied Wolfgang in English.

In May, Wolfgang and Nannerl gave a concert at the palace for a small gathering. The concert lasted from six p.m. to ten p.m. Wolfgang played his own compositions. Later he accompanied the Queen in a song and a flutist in a solo. He also played the organ. Again everyone was astonished.

Johann Christian Bach, the son of the great composer, Johann Sebastian Bach, was the Queen's music master. He said to Wolfgang, "How would you like to come and play for me sometime?"

"Thank you, I would like it very much," Wolfgang answered.

Soon, the 28-year-old Bach and the eight-year-

Johann Christian Bach came from a musical family, as did Mozart.

old boy were inseparable. Wolfgang learned a great deal from his older friend.

Wolfgang's success at court was such that Mr. Mozart decided his son should play for the general public. The boy gave his first subscription concert on June 5, 1764. Everyone praised him.

However, Wolfgang was still a little boy. One day when he was playing at a party, a kitten crossed the room. Wolfgang suddenly stopped playing, jumped from his chair, and ran to the

kitten. His father had a hard time bringing him back to the keyboard.

The Mozarts were in London over a year. While they were there Wolfgang heard several Italian operas. Opera started in Italy. It is a musical play with singers, ballet dancers, and an orchestra. Wolfgang loved it more than any other kind of music. "I want to write an opera!" he announced.

Wolfgang also went to symphony concerts. He

sat enchanted. He was quick to hear the slightest mistake, and knew at once which musician had made it. Now he wanted to compose a symphony too! But when could he find time to write a big composition for an entire orchestra? He and Papa were on the go all day with lessons, practicing, and performing. At night there were concerts, operas, and parties.

It almost seemed like luck when Papa came down with a cold and had to stay in bed.

"Nannerl," whispered Wolfgang, "I am going to write a symphony. Please remind me to give the horns plenty to do."

"But you are afraid of horns! Don't you remember? You used to run away and hide in Salzburg whenever you heard a horn."

"That's just it. I should keep them busy in an orchestra where they sound beautiful."

Wolfgang finished his first symphony when he was nine years old. It was performed in London. He wrote two more symphonies before leaving for Holland. He and his sister were to play there for the Prince and Princess.

The two children were tired. They had been gone from home for nearly three years. Traveling was not easy; lodgings were not always comfortable. It was hard to meet new people all the time and to entertain them hour after hour. In addition, the children had to practice every day. And Wolfgang composed music as well.

On their way to Holland, Nannerl and Wolfgang began to feel very sick. In Holland several doctors were called to treat them. Nannerl recovered quickly, but Wolfgang seemed to be unable to talk. As he lay in bed he would make the gestures of an orchestra conductor. He wept and chuckled but not a word came from his lips. His mother brought him some paper and he began to write some music. But his hand shook and his head fell to one side.

At last, one day, he spoke suddenly. "Mama, I want to go to the keyboard," he said.

Mama helped him to get up and walk to the instrument. From then on he began to get better. He composed six *Sonatas for Piano with Violin Accompaniment* and a symphony.

5. Did a Child Write This?

Mr. Mozart decided it was time to go back to Salzburg. The children were happy to be home at last.

When the Prince-Bishop saw Wolfgang's sonatas that had been printed in Paris, he said to Mr. Mozart, "Did a child write this? You must have helped him."

"Not at all, Your Highness."

"I cannot believe it. I shall have to see him do it myself."

The Prince-Bishop ordered Wolfgang to stay

in his palace for a week. He was shut up in a room all by himself, with paper and pen. No one was to come near him except the servants who brought him food.

The Prince-Bishop gave Wolfgang the words for a religious poem called an oratorio. He told him to write the music for it. Before the week ended Wolfgang had finished the oratorio. It covered 208 long sheets of music paper. The Prince-Bishop was amazed.

"And now," Papa said to Wolfgang, "let's get down to real work!"

This famous portrait of Mozart as he looked at eleven was painted by G. T. Helbling.

Wolfgang studied music with his father, and he practiced every day. He also studied Latin, French, and Italian. Soon he could read and write in these languages.

After eight months in Salzburg, Mr. Mozart asked the Prince-Bishop for a leave. Wolfgang was eleven years old now. Papa wanted to find a rich patron who would support Wolfgang while he composed and played. The patron would also introduce Wolfgang to noblemen and other rich people who were interested in the arts. In this way, Wolfgang could become famous as a performer and a composer.

The Prince-Bishop of Salzburg was also known as the Archbishop.

"We will go back to Vienna," Mr. Mozart said. "The Empress liked Wolfgang when we were there before. I am sure she will help us."

As soon as the family reached Vienna, Wolfgang came down with smallpox. He nearly died.

It was a bad beginning. What followed was no better. The Empress was no longer interested in Wolfgang's playing. A child prodigy had been exciting to her. A growing boy was not.

At last Mr. Mozart's friends persuaded the Emperor to ask Wolfgang to write an opera. "The boy will conduct the opera," the Emperor said. Papa was overjoyed. "You will be known everywhere, Wolfgang!" he said.

The opera was soon ready, but it was never performed. The older court musicians were jealous of young Wolfgang. They did not want a young boy as a conductor. At the rehearsal they played and sang out of tune on purpose. The Emperor tried to make them behave. But he was unsuccessful.

Wolfgang was very disappointed, but he kept busy. He composed three symphonies and a

Mozart's first opera, *La Finta Semplice* (The Pretended Simpleton), was written for Emperor Joseph II, shown above. Painting by Drouais.

Mass for church. The Emperor had him conduct the Mass in his own private chapel.

One day a famous physician, Dr. Mesmer, asked Wolfgang, "How would you like to write a one-act opera for me?"

"I would love it!"

"Good. The story is *Bastien and Bastienne*. It is all about shepherds and shepherdesses."

Wolfgang was delighted. In no time at all he

composed a small opera. It was performed in Dr. Mesmer's private theater, and was a great success.

Today people still like to hear the gay tunes of *Bastien and Bastienne*. Here is the beginning of the overture:

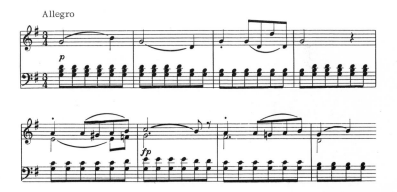

"Our trip to Vienna has not been a complete loss after all," Papa said, as they started back to Salzburg.

6. Viva L'Italia!

Wolfgang still had no patron and no court appointment.

"Wolfgang," Papa said, "we must go to Italy. The best musicians in the world live there. If you play and compose for them and they accept you, then everybody will know your worth. It will be easy to find a patron."

In early December 1769, father and son left for Italy. In order to save money, Nannerl and her mother stayed home.

Wolfgang loved Italy from the start. In each city, crowds of people came to hear him. He and his father were invited to stay at many rich people's homes. There were elegant dinners. Thirteen-year-old Wolfgang danced and fenced. He had a good time. Most important of all, he heard some wonderful music.

Finally they arrived in Rome, the most important city in Italy.

During Holy Week, father and son went to

the Sistine Chapel in the Vatican, the Pope's palace. They heard there a famous composition called *Miserere*. A composer named Allegri had written it a hundred years earlier. It was for the papal choir only. Choir singers and musicians were not allowed to take home any part of the music. If they ever did, they were to be severely punished.

Wolfgang sat in the chapel listening intently to the nine-part *Miserere*. As soon as it was over, he hurried back to the inn and began to write.

"What are you doing?" Papa inquired.

"Writing down the *Miserere*."

"Can you remember all of it?"

"Yes, I believe so. However, I want to make sure. Can we go back to the Sistine Chapel on Good Friday and hear the *Miserere* again?"

They did. Wolfgang hid his music paper in his hat. As he listened once more to the performance he checked his manuscript secretly. He found it quite perfect.

It became known that young Mozart had

written down all the *Miserere* from memory. He was asked to bring it to the Vatican. What was going to happen to Wolfgang? Mama and Nannerl wrote worried letters. Papa wrote back:

"We both had a good laugh when we read your letter. There is nothing to worry about. It is taken quite another way. All Rome knows about it. Even the Pope himself."

In fact the Pope was far from angry. He even gave Wolfgang a special gold medal, and made him *Knight of the Order of the Golden Spur*. From then on, Wolfgang could be addressed as *Signor Cavaliere* which meant Sir Knight. A fourteen-year-old musician had never before been honored in this way. Papa was very proud when people bowed in front of his young son and called him Signor Cavaliere Mozart.

"Wolfgang," he said, "I want you to wear the medal all the time. And from now on you must sign all your letters *Signor Cavaliere Mozart.*"

Wolfgang tried to please Papa. But he wrote to Nannerl:

"Title and medal will go the way of all
our other souvenirs—that is, in the
chest!"

At last the time came for Wolfgang to be tested by some of the best Italian musicians. A group of them invited him to come to Bologna and try out for membership in the famous Academy of Bologna.

This painting of Mozart wearing the golden cross was said by his father to be a very good likeness of Wolfgang when he was 21.

Wolfgang was given a theme from an old church songbook and locked in a room, all by himself.

"You have three hours to compose part of a Mass on that theme," the musicians told him.

Within half an hour Wolfgang got up and called, "I have finished!"

"What!" they cried. "Such a short time! Let us see what you have done."

These great musicians examined Wolfgang's work very carefully. They looked for the slightest mistake. Then, they shook their heads and said, "It is truly wonderful!"

They voted to let him become a member. Wolfgang was the youngest composer ever to belong to the Academy of Bologna.

The Mozarts then went on to Milan. Milan's Governor-General had asked Wolfgang to write an opera on a story called *Mithridate, King of Pontus*. It was performed the day after Christmas 1770. Fourteen-year-old Wolfgang conducted the opera.

The public clapped and clapped. They shouted, "Bravo! Long live the little master!" The opera was repeated twenty times that winter.

Leopold Mozart's joy knew no bounds. "Wolfgang," he said, "people love your music. The world's outstanding musical authorities have accepted you. Now it should be easy to find you a rich patron."

"Yes, Papa," Wolfgang answered happily.

The trip to Italy had been a great success. His playing and composing had been admired everywhere.

Equally important, he had learned a lot. He had heard the world's greatest singers and musicians, and studied the works of some outstanding composers.

"Papa," Wolfgang said, "I am no longer a child prodigy. I am now a man."

He began to sign his compositions "Wolfgang Amadeus Mozart." He had changed "Gottlieb" into the Latin word "Amadeus."

7. First Great Works

When Wolfgang finally returned to Salzburg, he was sixteen years old. That year the Prince-Bishop died. His death was a great blow to the Mozart family. The Prince-Bishop had been their good friend. He had granted Mr. Mozart many a long leave from the court orchestra so that he could travel with Wolfgang. The new Prince-Bishop was haughty and stingy.

Leopold Mozart hoped to be made conductor of the court orchestra. But the Prince-Bishop appointed an Italian. Mr. Mozart was made assistant conductor and Wolfgang court composer. Wolfgang's salary was very small, about that of a servant.

The Prince-Bishop had no appreciation of music. Wolfgang disliked composing for him. Young Mozart amused himself by writing music for all the balls in town. Wolfgang still loved dancing, and the Salzburg girls liked him very much.

Leopold Mozart tried to get a leave to travel again. The Prince-Bishop was angry. "What kind of a conductor are you?" he said. "You are always on the road with your son. Who is paying you? I am! You and your son are to stay right here."

Luckily, Wolfgang got a letter from the Ruler of Bavaria, Elector Maximilian Joseph. He asked Wolfgang to compose an opera. The story was *La Finta Giardiniera,* (The Pretend Garden Girl). It had a silly plot, but Wolfgang did not care. The important thing for him was the music. The Elector invited Wolfgang to be present in Munich at the opening performance. The Prince-Bishop had to let Wolfgang and his father go.

The opera was a huge success. Wolfgang wrote Mama:

"There was a frightful din of clapping and cries of *viva maestro!* after each aria."

The Prince-Bishop arrived in Munich. Everybody talked to him about the opera. People said, "Congratulations, Your Highness! You have a young genius at your service." The Prince-Bishop only shrugged his shoulders.

Wolfgang would have liked to stay in Munich and work for the Elector of Bavaria. But he was not offered a job. Soon the day came when he and his father had to go back to Salzburg.

Wolfgang threw himself into composing. Five years went by. During this time he wrote his first outstanding works. Among them were *Five Violin Concerti*, the *Haffner Serenade* and the *Piano Concerto in E Flat Major*. Still the Prince-Bishop paid little attention to him.

Wolfgang was not patient like his father. He

Violin Concerto in A Major

was 21 years old now. He was gay and bursting with life and talent. He felt he could not remain in Salzburg any longer. He wrote to the Prince-Bishop:

"May Your Highness authorize your humble servant to offer his resignation....

The very humble servant
of Your Highness,
Wolfgang Amadeus Mozart."

"How are you going to live?" Papa asked. "A low salary is better than none at all."

Wolfgang laughed. "I will go to Germany and France. I am sure I will be able to earn some money there."

"All right. You should try your luck in bigger

places than Salzburg. But this time you will have to travel alone. I must remain here and earn some money for the family."

Although Papa could not travel with Wolfgang, he planned everything for the trip. He even looked after Wolfgang's clothes and luggage. He was worried because Wolfgang was not very businesslike. Finally, he decided Mama would go with her son. Papa and Nannerl would stay home together.

A letter written by Mozart in 1789.

8. A Terrible Loss

At last the day of departure came. Wolfgang and his mother were in the carriage. Papa, holding the carriage door, still poured out advice. "Be careful, Wolfgang. Watch what you eat. Take plenty of rest. Beware of pretty girls. Write me everything. Everything!"

Wolfgang promised. He loved Papa so much. When he was little he used to say, "After God, Papa comes next!"

Wolfgang enjoyed riding in carriages. As they

Mozart's piano in the foreground and his traveling clavier in the background can be seen today in the Mozart Museum in Salzburg.

bumped along all sorts of musical ideas ran through his mind. Some made him laugh aloud. Some made him sad. His mother kept very quiet. She knew that her gentle son could get angry if he were disturbed. He made up entire compositions in his head. Later, in an inn, he would write them down from memory.

In Augsburg, Wolfgang went to see the new piano made by Mr. Stein. Wolfgang sat down to play. How beautiful! Mr. Stein was delighted. This piano was a great improvement over the other keyboard instruments. Wolfgang's playing helped make the piano popular.

From Augsburg, Mama and Wolfgang went to Mannheim on the Rhine River. It was a gay city and a center of culture. Wolfgang met many musicians. He went to one party after another. He even met a girl he fell in love with for a time.

Wolfgang longed to remain in Mannheim. The ruler there loved the arts and sciences. He had a theater and a famous orchestra. Wolfgang was invited to play at the court. But there was no

Aloysia Weber, the girl Mozart met and fell in love with in Mannheim, was a gifted singer.

Portrait of Marie Antoinette by Vigee Le Brun.

regular job for him. Sadly, he said good-bye to his new friends and started for Paris.

Paris was not the same city Wolfgang had known as a child. The young King Louis XVI was married to Marie Antoinette. She was the princess that Wolfgang had played with in Vienna when he was six years old. Marie Antoinette was not interested in helping young musicians. There were rich people who helped composers, but Paris was full of gifted musicians starting their careers. The noblemen did not realize Mozart was outstanding.

Finally, Wolfgang was asked to compose a symphony. The *Paris Symphony* was well received. Wolfgang wrote to his father:

> ". . . the audience was quite carried away — and there was a tremendous burst of applause . . . I was so happy that as soon as the Symphony was over, I went off to the Palais Royal, where I had a large sherbet, said the rosary as I had vowed to do, and went home."

In spite of this success, Wolfgang was soon forgotten. He had to try other ways to attract attention. During their first visit in Paris, the Mozarts had made friends with a man who was interested in music. His name was Mr. Grimm. He thought Wolfgang should give music lessons to members of the nobility. That way Wolfgang would become better known. Besides he would be earning money, which he needed badly.

Mr. Grimm (Baron Freidrich von Grimm), who was Mozart's friend, was a writer and critic.

Wolfgang began to give lessons all over Paris. It was very tiring. One of his pupils in composition was a Duke's daughter. She did not want to work. Wolfgang said to Mama, "I do everything I can, but she is stupid and lazy."

The girl played the harp, and her father played the flute. The Duke asked Wolfgang to write some music for them to play together. Wolfgang composed the *C Major Concerto for Flute and Harp*. The Duke gave him very little money.

Wolfgang was angry. He told Mama, "I sent it back with the message that I did not want to rob him of his money."

Quick anger and pride were two of Wolfgang's faults. He knew his own worth and felt he deserved proper recognition. He could be quite rude when he felt that people did not appreciate him.

Wolfgang wrote several other compositions. Among them was the *Piano Sonata in A Major* with the famous Turkish march.

Wolfgang was making very little money, and he was not getting any better known. He kept telling Mama, "One of these days, our luck is bound to change."

Mama had not been feeling well. She tried to hide it from her son. Then suddenly she fell very ill. "Get me a German doctor," she told Wolfgang.

Wolfgang did. But the doctor could not save Mama. She died in her son's arms.

Poor heartbroken Wolfgang was alone in Paris. Mr. Grimm invited him to stay with him. But the two men had different ideas about Wolfgang's career. Mr. Grimm wanted Wolfgang to be more businesslike and to flatter important people. He wrote Leopold Mozart, "Wolfgang is too kindhearted, not active enough, all too easily deceived, too little concerned with the means that can lead him to success."

Papa wrote Wolfgang and begged him to listen to Mr. Grimm. But Wolfgang was not willing to kowtow to people with title or money. Already in America, as well as France, people were talking about the rights of the individual. Young people wanted to be appreciated for what they were, not for their social position. Old Mr. Grimm could not understand it. He decided Wolfgang should leave his house.

Just then news came from Salzburg. The conductor of the court orchestra had died, also the court composer. The Prince-Bishop offered the job of conductor to Leopold Mozart. It was what he had wanted for so long. But there was a condition. Leopold Mozart could have the job only if his son promised to be court composer and organist.

Wolfgang was crestfallen. Return to Salzburg? How could he? He could not stand the Prince-Bishop. And there was no opera or theater in Salzburg.

Leopold Mozart wrote, "We shall be better off at home than anywhere else. It is less expensive to live here." He added that the Prince-Bishop was willing to let Wolfgang travel whenever he wanted to go away to produce an opera.

Finally, Wolfgang accepted the offer. He left at once for Salzburg.

9. The Price of Freedom

It was a sad family reunion without Mama. They all wept. Papa and Nannerl tried to make things warm and cozy for Wolfgang. There was roast chicken for dinner, a great treat in those days.

Wolfgang began to work hard. He wanted to help support his father and Nannerl. He composed music for the Prince-Bishop's church. He also wrote symphonies, and some light music—divertimenti and serenades. He kept trying to please the Prince-Bishop.

But the Prince-Bishop had not changed. He never lost a chance to humiliate Wolfgang. "The bright young man has had to come back and work for me," he would boast.

People in Salzburg liked Wolfgang, but his music sounded strange to them. "When I play in Salzburg," Wolfgang said, "or when my compositions are performed, the audience might just as well be chairs or tables."

One day a letter came from the Elector of Bavaria. Wolfgang was overjoyed. "Nannerl!

This famous painting of the Mozart family, done by J. N. dela Croce, hangs in the Mozart Museum.

Papa! I have been asked to write an opera for the Munich Carnival! The story is from Greek mythology. It is called *Idomeneo*."

For three months Wolfgang worked night and day. Then he hurried to Munich for the rehearsal. *Idomeneo* was a success. Papa and Nannerl, who were there for the performance, were very happy and so was Wolfgang. The three of them stayed for the Carnival and had a marvelous time.

Meanwhile, the Empress of Austria had died, and the Prince-Bishop had gone to Vienna to pay his respects to the new Emperor. When the Mozarts got back to Salzburg, Wolfgang was told to meet the Prince-Bishop in Vienna at once. The Prince-Bishop wanted to be seen in style with his servants, two cooks, a baker, two valets, his treasurer, and his musician, Wolfgang Amadeus Mozart. Wolfgang was angry. But what could he do?

In Vienna, the Prince-Bishop was at his worst. He made Wolfgang eat in the kitchen

with the servants. While he was in Vienna, Wolfgang had hoped to become better known and even make a little money. But the Prince-Bishop made him refuse all invitations.

The new Emperor went to his summer residence. He did not invite the Prince-Bishop there as he disliked him. The Prince-Bishop felt insulted and decided to return to Salzburg at once. He told Wolfgang to leave immediately. That night when Wolfgang was still there, the Prince-Bishop shouted angrily, "Why haven't you left?"

"I tried to leave tonight. But there were no seats on the stagecoach."

"What? You are the laziest, the most careless boy I know! No one serves me so badly. Go home tomorrow, or I will stop your salary. Do you hear me? Get out!"

Wolfgang returned to his inn. He was deeply hurt. Later, he went to tell the Prince-Bishop that he was resigning. He never had a chance. The Prince-Bishop's secretary kicked him out the door.

Wolfgang wrote his father all that had happened. He added, "I shall send you a little money by the next mail. I hope that this will convince you that I will not starve in Vienna."

Surely Papa would understand! But Papa did not. He feared that the angry Prince-Bishop would dismiss him too. Then what would become of the family? Papa begged Wolfgang to apologize to the Prince-Bishop and ask humbly to be taken back.

Wolfgang was appalled. Papa, whom he adored, was against him!

This was a turning point in Wolfgang's life. He had to make his own decisions. He had to be free even if it meant hurting Papa's feelings deeply.

Wolfgang stayed in Vienna.

10. The Struggle

How was Mozart going to make a living? Piano lessons, that was the answer. He rose every day at six A.M. and wrote music until his pupils came. He taught until two P.M. After lunch he gave more lessons. In the evening he composed again until well into the night. Freedom gave him boundless energy. However, freedom did not make him rich. He received only six ducats for twelve lessons. That is about a dollar a lesson, today.

Yet it was not all work. Rich people in Vienna invited Mozart to their homes. He took part in Sunday afternoon musicals at noblemen's houses. There, he also heard a lot of outstanding music. Handel and Bach were very popular in Vienna then.

The Emperor wanted Mozart to play at court with a well-known Italian musician. It would be a contest. Which musician played the best?

The Italian played first. Then the Emperor

told Mozart, "Come now, fire away!" Mozart's playing enchanted everybody. The Italian musician wrote to a friend about Mozart. "I had until this time never heard piano playing which was so full of spirit and grace."

The Emperor wanted Mozart to write a comic opera with a Turkish background. Mozart composed the *Abduction from the Seraglio*. It had rich and lovely music, but it was too new for the people of Vienna.

Friends told Mozart, "Write something popular. Then you will be successful and make money."

"I would rather go hungry," Mozart said. "I will not give the people what they want. I will give them only my best."

Mozart was living with a family called the Webers. Before long he wrote to his father about one of the daughters, Constanze:

> "I must make you acquainted with the character of my Constanze.... Her great beauty consists of a pair of sparkling black eyes and a pretty figure.... She has the best heart in all the world. I love her with my whole soul and she does me."

Papa was thoroughly displeased. He did not want Wolfgang to get married until he was more successful. He felt that marriage now would lead to nothing but poverty. Twenty-six-year-old Wolfgang pleaded and pleaded. He did not want to go against dear Papa's wishes.

Constanze von Weber, who became Mozart's wife.

In the end he married Constanze without his father's consent.

Mozart and Constanze found an apartment in one of Vienna's crooked old streets. It was fun to have their own home. They were poor, but Mozart felt sure success would come.

Constanze had little sense about money. She was not a good housekeeper, though she did her best. Mozart himself did not know how to manage financial matters. He was overly generous with friends in need.

When money did come in, the Mozarts bought chicken and wine and invited all their friends. One of their best friends was the great composer Haydn.

Haydn was a kind man. Although he was 50, he was not one bit jealous of young Mozart. On the contrary, he always praised him highly. Once he told Papa, "I tell you before God and as a man of honor, that your son is the greatest composer of whom I have heard."

Often, Haydn and Mozart played their own compositions for each other. Mozart admired

Joseph Haydn influenced Mozart's compositional style and also was influenced himself by Mozart.

Haydn's music very much. He dedicated his famous *Six Strings Quartets* to Haydn.

Two years went by. On September 21, 1784, a son was born to the Mozarts. They named the baby Karl.

The Mozarts moved to a larger apartment. They invited Papa to visit them. Nannerl had married a nobleman, and had moved to another town. She seldom wrote, and Papa was lonesome.

Papa was happy to see his son working so hard. During the past two years Mozart had

written many compositions, including works for the piano, the violin, the horn, and the viola. He had also written one symphony and nine piano concerti. All these works are still played and loved today. The *D Minor Piano Concerto* is the best known. The *C Minor* is one of the most beautiful piano concerti ever composed.

Mozart played two of his concerti at a concert. Papa wrote to Nannerl:

"They were *magnifiques*—magnificent."

11. Ups and Downs

Wolfgang wanted to write another opera. "Opera to me," he once said, "comes before anything else."

He decided to base his opera on a new French play called *The Marriage of Figaro.*

This was a daring story in Mozart's time. It made fun of the nobility. Mozart had to have the Emperor's permission to have the opera performed. This proved difficult, but finally the Emperor gave his consent.

This old engraving by Choubard shows Figaro as
he was first played in Vienna.

May 1, 1786 was the opening night. The opera house was packed. Mozart conducted the orchestra from his seat at the piano.

Most operas then were light and formal. The music did not try to say anything important. Mozart, however, had created a real drama. He had fitted the music to each character and made his people come to life. This was new. People loved it. They wanted to hear the arias or songs

The program from the first performance of *The Marriage of Figaro* was elaborately decorated.

A scene from *The Marriage of Figaro*. Although the opera was not a success in Vienna, it has become Mozart's best-known opera.

over and over again. The performance lasted twice as long as it should have.

Mozart had great hopes for the future. But some people were jealous of him. They persuaded the Emperor to favor another composer. *The Marriage of Figaro* played only nine times.

Mozart was worried about money. He was in debt. Suddenly, news came that *The Marriage of Figaro* was being produced in Prague. This was the capital of Bohemia, the country now called Czechoslovakia.

In the foreground is the house in Vienna where
Mozart wrote *The Marriage of Figaro*. Austrians
call it *Figarohaus*.

Mozart and his wife left Karl with a nurse. They hurried to Prague and went to the opera house. The place was crowded. Soon people in the audience began to whisper to each other, "Mozart! Look! There he is. Yes, it is he!"

After the overture everybody rose and cheered him, "Viva Maestro! Viva Maestro!" He got up, bowed and bowed again. The performance was a tremendous success. Afterwards, people flocked around Mozart. *Figaro* had taken Prague by a storm. Mozart wrote to a friend:

> "For in the city of Prague nothing is talked about but *Figaro*, nothing is played but *Figaro*, nothing whistled or sung on the streets but *Figaro*, no opera so crowded as *Figaro*, everywhere, everything is *Figaro*. All this is indeed very flattering to me."

There are many famous songs in *Figaro*. One of them is *Voi che sapete* (You know what love is). The overture of *Figaro* is one of the world's most popular melodies.

Mozart's stay in Prague was a triumph. Before he left, the director of the opera asked him to write another opera and paid him in advance for it. That opera was *Don Giovanni*. It is about a man who wants to win the love of every pretty woman he meets.

Back in Vienna, Mozart set to work on *Don Giovanni*. Often he took his music paper with him to a bowling green. While waiting to play, he sat at a table and wrote. Suddenly, one of his partners would yell, "Mozart! Your turn!" Mozart would jump up from the table, throw the balls and then go back to his writing.

He was happy composing but there was sad news from Salzburg. Papa was ill. In the spring he died. Mozart was heartbroken. Papa had been his first music teacher. He had also been his manager for a long time. Father and son

had not always understood one another, yet each had loved the other dearly.

Mozart went on writing *Don Giovanni*. At the same time he composed many other works famous today. *Eine Kleine Nachtmüsik*, is one of his most popular orchestral compositions. It has a beautiful haunting melody.

One day, as Mozart was busy composing, a stout, unattractive looking youth came to see him.

"I have heard you play the piano, Mr. Mozart. I would like to take lessons from you."

Mozart looked at the unexpected visitor coolly. He thought he was just another young man who knew nothing about music.

He pointed to the piano, "Go to the piano and play something. Anything."

The youth began to play. Mozart was astonished. He went into the next room where some of his friends were sitting. "This young man should be watched. He will soon make a noise in the world." Then he came back and said to the youth, "I am sorry, I did not catch your name when you came in."

"My name is Ludwig van Beethoven."

This was the man who was to become one of the world's greatest composers. Beethoven did not study with Mozart because Mozart was too tired to give lessons. He had no strength left except to finish *Don Giovanni*.

An old painting of Beethoven playing for Mozart.

Mozart and his wife went to Prague. Mozart had all the music written except the overture. The night before the opening, he and Constanze were at a friend's home. Mozart sat at the piano and played. Suddenly someone said, "What about the overture for *Don Giovanni?*"

Mozart jumped up. "Indeed! It will be done at once."

As he started upstairs, he turned to his wife. "Please, dear," he said, "mix me a bowl of punch and come and sit beside me. You will tell me fairy tales while I write."

That was the way he liked to work. Everything was already composed in his head. He had only to put it down on paper from memory. He wrote fast. He did not have to cross out or rewrite anything. The night wore on. Constanze told him one fairy tale after another to keep him awake.

Copies of the overture had to be made for every musician in the orchestra. The printers worked furiously to get them ready. There was no time for a rehearsal.

Before going on the stage, Mozart told the

This unfinished portrait of Mozart by J. Lange is
thought to have been done in 1782 or 1783.

members of the orchestra, "I am perfectly sure
that the Prague orchestra can play a new overture at sight."

They did. The performance was so good that
nobody guessed the musicians were playing the
overture for the first time.

Don Giovanni was very popular in Prague.

The richness and variety of its music make it one of the world's greatest operas.

The Mozarts returned to Vienna. The court composer had died. At long last the Emperor offered Mozart the position. Gluck, the former court composer, had been paid 2,000 florins a year. The Emperor offered Mozart only 800, or about $400 in today's money. Mozart accepted because he needed money badly. Constanze was not well. Karl had to be educated. And Mozart was deeply in debt.

12. Dark Days

On December 7, 1787 another baby was born. The Mozarts named her Theresia.

"We shall move to the country," Mozart said. "It will be better for the children."

"What about your duties as court composer?" Constanze asked.

"All the Emperor wants me to do is compose dances for the court balls. I can do that anywhere. I am paid too much for what I do, and too little for what I am capable of doing."

They liked the country. Above all, it was cheaper than Vienna. Yet they could not get out of debt. Mozart had to keep borrowing from a friend of his. It wounded his pride, but it could not be helped.

In the spring of 1788, there was a ray of hope. The Emperor wanted *Don Giovanni* to be given in Vienna. It was a failure.

The Emperor said, "My dear Mozart, the opera is divine. But such music is no meat for my Viennese."

"Give them time to chew on it, Your Majesty," Mozart replied.

Indeed, there was so much in that opera! It was tragic and it was comic. It was funny and it was sad, just like life. But the Viennese did not recognize the greatness of *Don Giovanni* until years later.

Mozart felt discouraged. In addition to his failure and worries, grief came to the family. The baby Theresia died in June.

That summer, in the midst of his gloom, Mozart composed his three most outstanding symphonies — 39, 40, 41. Each is different in mood, each is great. The *G Minor Symphony*, Number 40, is considered the perfect model for symphonies. It begins with a heartbreaking melody:

The following spring a nobleman invited Mozart to go with him to Berlin. "I will introduce you to King Frederic II of Prussia," the nobleman said.

Mozart was delighted. He loved being on the road again. He was full of hope. Perhaps this time he would find an understanding patron.

They stopped in Dresden, and Mozart played for the court. He received a snuff-box. A snuff-box! He opened it and found 100 ducats! He hurried to write Constanze all about it. He added:

> "Dear little wife, I have a number of requests to make. I beg you: not to be melancholy, to take care of your health and to beware of the spring breezes, not to go walking alone. . . .
>
> Now farewell, dearest, most beloved! Please remember that every night before going to bed I talk to your portrait for a good half-hour and do the same when I awake. . . .
>
> O Stru! Stri! I kiss and squeeze you 1095060437082 times . . . and I am ever your most faithful husband and friend. . . ."

In Berlin, Mozart was entertained by the King of Prussia. He had known about Mozart and was eager to hear him. The King enjoyed Mozart's playing very much, but he did not offer him an

appointment to the court. However, he did ask Mozart to write six quartets and some piano sonatas. This was better than nothing. But it was not enough to solve the Mozarts' financial problems.

Mozart returned to Vienna and went to see the Emperor. "How about writing a comic opera?" the Emperor said. He gave Mozart 200 ducats in advance. Perhaps good times were coming back. Mozart set to work eagerly on the new opera, *Cosi fan tutte*.

But Constanze did not feel well. One day she seemed better, and the next she was worse.

The doctor ordered special herb teas, leeches, sticky medicines, and ants' eggs. They all cost money. Mozart was frantic. "I shall give some concerts," he said. The subscription list came back with only one name. Everyone was out of town.

The doctor said, "Mr. Mozart, your wife will have to go to a health resort."

Mozart had to borrow money again, and Constanze left for a resort called Baden. Karl was away in boarding school.

Constanze's health improved. She returned, and the Mozarts then moved into the cheapest apartment they could find. Moving was easy. Besides the piano and Mozart's pet canary, there were only a few pieces of furniture. Most of it had been sold to pay debts.

Cosi fan tutte was performed in January 1790. It was fairly well received. A number of performances were planned for that winter. Unfortunately, the Emperor died. The court went into mourning and all performances were cancelled.

Perhaps Mozart would get a better position now. He wanted to be the conductor of the court orchestra. He was so worried about money that he had no pride left. He asked the new Emperor for the job.

The new Emperor did not care about music. Nothing came from Mozart's request. Again he had to borrow money from his friend. In his letter he added:

"I have only two pupils. I should like to have eight. So please endeavour to let it be known that I do not object to giving lessons."

The rest of the year dragged on. Constanze was ill again. Mozart himself did not feel well. He was so worried that he could not work. The only thing that cheered him was the singing of his canary.

The next winter was bitterly cold. A friend dropped in at the Mozarts'. He found Mozart dancing with Constanze.

"What? Teaching your wife how to dance?"

Mozart laughed. "My dear friend, we are only warming ourselves. We are freezing and cannot afford to buy any wood for the fire."

The friend went out and brought back some of his own wood. Later, when he could, Mozart repaid him.

In spite of worry and illness, Mozart went on composing. He wrote outstanding works for string and for clarinet. For the piano he composed the great *Concerto in B Flat Major*. The music sings of his unhappiness and misery. Then at the end, it is light and carefree. It is as if Mozart had accepted his fate.

13. Mozart, Music Magician

Soon Mozart was busy on another opera, *The Magic Flute.* A friend gave him the idea for the plot. This friend Emanuel Schikaneder produced plays. He knew that people liked humor, romance, and stories of faraway places.

Schikaneder found a perfect story in a book of Oriental folktales. He told Mozart about it.

"Pamina, a beautiful girl, is the daughter of the Queen of the Night. She is loved by Prince Tamino. But she is kidnapped and shut up in an Egyptian palace. Prince Tamino sets out to rescue her. The Queen of the Night gives him a magic flute which will protect him. Tamino has many adventures, until, finally, thanks to the magic flute, he triumphs over all obstacles. He frees Pamina, and they live together happily ever after.

"How do you like it, Mozart?"

"Very much, indeed!"

"We shall have birds, fire, water, and even lions on the stage!" Schikaneder said.

Mozart was very excited. He began to compose the music. His mind worked very fast. But his body was worn out. He began to feel that he was not going to live much longer.

An engraving by A. Borckmann shows a festive dinner at Emanuel Schikaneder's home. Schikaneder (standing) is proposing a toast to Mozart (in the foreground).

He was only 35, but the struggle had been too great. He had been working since he was six. Throughout his married life he had to fight for his daily bread and for that of his family. Above all, he suffered because he was not recognized as the outstanding composer he knew he was.

He thought a great deal about death. He wrote:

"I never lie down in my bed without considering that as young as I am, perhaps I may on the morrow be no more."

One day, as he was busy composing, a stranger knocked at the door. The man was dressed in dark gray. He was tall, quiet, and mysterious.

He handed Mozart a letter. The letter had no signature. The anonymous writer asked Mozart to set a fee for a requiem, a composition for a funeral. There was one condition. Mozart was not to try to discover the name of this unknown patron. Later the messenger would call for the composition.

Many portraits have been painted of Mozart, including this one in a very romantic style.

Mozart accepted. The visitor left. Who was he?

Mozart began composing passages for the *Requiem*. He worked on it at the same time he wrote *The Magic Flute*.

That autumn the Emperor was to be crowned King of Bohemia. Mozart was asked to write an opera for the coronation.

He and Constanze left for Prague. As they settled in the carriage, the mysterious, tall stranger suddenly appeared at the window.

"What about the *Requiem*?" he asked.

"I'll finish it as soon as I am back," said Mozart. The stranger bowed and was gone.

Mozart was upset. Who was the *Requiem* for? He feared it was for himself. Had he known it, the story was quite simple. A rich countess had died. Her husband was an amateur musician, but he was not skillful enough to compose a requiem. So he asked Mozart to write one. It would appear under the Count's name. Ghost-writing was common at that time.

Mozart and Constanze stayed in Prague for the coronation. Then they hurried back home to their new son. Franz Xaver had been born earlier in the year.

Soon Mozart completed *The Magic Flute*. The opera was performed on September 30, 1791. It had everything—fantasy, charm, and romance. People loved it. The orchestration was rich and the arias beautiful.

Mozart was happy. At long last, Vienna appreciated him! But it was too late. His health was broken. Still working on the *Requiem,* he wrote to a friend in Italy:

> "I am on the point of dying. My end has come before I was able to profit by my talent. No one can count his days; one must resign oneself. What Providence determines will be done. I close now. Before me lies my funeral song. I must not leave it unfinished."

Mozart felt worse and worse. Constanze called a doctor. But there was nothing he could do.

In October, Mozart felt a little better. He composed his immortal *A major Concerto for clarinet*. This is Mozart's last finished composition.

Now he worked feverishly on the *Requiem*. He began to fear that he could not finish it. He was in bed most of the time.

Soon he could not get up at all. The doctor brought other doctors. Nobody seemed to know exactly what the trouble was. To make matters worse, Constanze was ill again and could not look after him.

Mozart felt worse and worse. He could no longer bear the singing of his beloved canary. "Please take it away," he said sadly.

While he lay ill in bed, people were crowding Vienna's Opera House to hear *The Magic Flute*.

A watercolor of a scene from *The Magic Flute*.

In the evening, some pupils and musicians came to see Mozart. He glanced at his watch. "The first act of *The Magic Flute* is just ending," he said. A little later he announced, "Now comes the grand aria for the Queen of the Night." He tried to beat time with his hands. In a little while, with a faint voice, he began to sing the bird catcher's song.

The bird-ie catch-er   I am, yes, al-ways hap-py, hey-hey! oops-la - la!

This is the house in which Mozart died.

On the fourth day of December, Mozart was very weak. Still he tried to work on the unfinished *Requiem*. He asked some of his friends to sing it. They did. As they came to the Latin words *lacrimosa dies,* meaning "day of tears," Mozart suddenly became more ill. That night, one of his pupils stayed with him. A little after midnight, Mozart turned his head to the wall and closed his eyes forever. It was December 5, 1791.

The funeral took place the following day.

Constanze was too sick to leave her bed. A few friends went to the church. Then they started to follow the coffin to the cemetery. But the snow and wind became so fierce that they turned back. Mozart was taken alone to his final rest.

Later, when Constanze went to look for the grave of her beloved husband, no one could tell her where it was. He had been buried in an unmarked grave for poor people.

A monument to Mozart by Victor Tilgner.

Wolfgang Amadeus Mozart's position is unique in music history. As a child he was a prodigy; as an adult he was one of the world's greatest composers.

Mozart's musical ideas poured out of him in endless streams. He composed as naturally and easily as he breathed. He left more than 600 compositions, including operas, symphonies, concerti, serenades, divertimenti, dance tunes, songs, sonatas, church compositions, and chamber music.

While he was alive, Mozart's genius was not recognized. Starving, burdened with debts, his health shattered, he died in complete poverty and went alone to his unknown final resting place.

Now, nearly 200 years later, his music is heard day and night, and is produced all over the world. In concert halls, homes, cars, planes and spaceships, everyone enjoys the great art of Mozart, music magician.

Mozart's Music

Some Listening Choices

Available on Records

Operas

       The Magic Flute
       Don Giovanni
       The Marriage of Figaro

Symphonies

       K.550   No. 40 – G Minor
       K.551   No. 41 – C Major (Jupiter)
       K.543   No. 39 – E Flat Major

Concerti

Piano	K.466	D Minor
	K.491	C Minor
	K.482	E Flat Major
	K.595	B Flat Major
Violin	K.219	A Major
	K.218	D Major
	K.216	G Major
Horn	K.412	D Major
	K.417	E Flat Major
	K.447	E Flat Major
	K.495	E Flat Major
Flute	K.313	G Major
Bassoon	K.191	B Flat Major
Clarinet	K.622	A Major

Piano Sonatas, Variations, Fantasies

K.545	C Major
K.332	F Major
K.331	A Major (The Turkish)
K.283	G Major
K.310	A Minor
K.448	D Major for Two Pianos
K.475	Fantasy in C Minor
K.265	"Ah! Vous dirai-je Maman"

Serenades

K.525	Eine Kleine Nachtmüsik
K.361	B Flat Major for Twelve Wind Instruments

Church Music

K.626	Requiem (unfinished)
K.618	Ave Verum Corpus
K.165	Exultate

Chamber Music

K.421	D Minor)
K.428	E Flat Major)
K.458	B Flat Major) "Hayden Quartets
K.464	A Major) for Strings"
K.465	C Major)
K.516	G Minor – Quintet for Strings
K.581	Quintet for Strings and Clarinet
K.299	C Major – Duet for Flute and Harp

Glossary

adagio — tempo mark meaning very slow

allegretto — tempo mark meaning moderately fast

allegro — tempo mark meaning fast

andante — tempo mark meaning slow

aria — an elaborate composition for solo voice (occasionally a duet) with instrumental accompaniment that is part of an opera or oratorio

chord — the simultaneous sounding of three or more tones related to each other harmonically

clavier — a stringed instrument having a keyboard, like a piano

concerto — a composition for a solo instrument, piano, violin, flute, etc., accompanied by an orchestra

divertimento — a light work in several movements for a small instrumental group

larghetto — tempo mark meaning slow and majestic

mass — the main Roman Catholic service, sometimes sung

minuet — graceful three-beat dance music sometimes used as the third movement in a sonata

molto allegro — tempo mark meaning very fast

opera — a drama or play which is in general sung throughout to the accompaniment of an orchestra

oratorio — a musical setting of a dramatic or epic text, often on a sacred subject, for voices and instruments

overture — instrumental music composed as an introduction to an opera, oratorio, or other vocal work

presto — tempo mark meaning very fast; faster than allegro

requiem — a mass for the dead

serenade — a light instrumental form of evening entertainment music for outdoor performance

sonata — a musical composition built on two themes (subjects), in three or four movements alternatively fast and slow, written mostly for piano, violin, or cello

symphony — a lengthy musical work for full orchestra, usually built like a sonata in three or four movements with various rhythms

tempo marks — indications of the speed of a composition or a section

tutti — indication on orchestral works of the passages to be played by the whole orchestra, as distinct from those of the soloist

Index

Claire Huchet Bishop, was raised in Le Havre, France, and studied at the Sorbonne. Story-telling was a favorite avocation in the Huchet family, and Claire began telling stories at the first French Children's Library in Paris. Later, she told stories at the New York Public Library and began to write them down as well.

Mrs. Bishop's first published work was poetry, followed by articles, reviews, and books for both adults and children. Her books have been translated in several languages, and she has contributed to such magazines as *The Saturday Review, The Commonweal, The Fellowship of Reconciliation,* and *Land Reborn.*

Mrs. Bishop's avocation is music, which led her to write the life story of Mozart. Although she makes frequent visits to her native land, the author makes her home in New York City.

Paul Frame, whose charming drawings illustrate this biography of Mozart, is himself a person of rare charm and warmth. He enjoys the challenge of bringing forth the personalities of characters in a story, and toward this end he spends a great deal of time, thought, and research. Besides his talent for capturing the flavor of a book, he is meticulous about accuracy of details.

Born in Riderwood, Maryland, Mr. Frame was raised and educated in various parts of the country. He and his wife and two daughters now live in New York City.

Mr. Frame does fashion and advertising illustration, and he has illustrated over 50 books. Among them are Garrard's *Mississippi Steamboat Days, David Glasgow Farragut: Our First Admiral,* and *The Game of Football.*

Paul Frame, whose charming drawings illustrate this biography of Mozart, is himself a person of rare charm and warmth. He enjoys the challenge of bringing forth the personalities of characters in a story, and toward this end he spends a great deal of time, thought, and research. Besides his talent for capturing the flavor of a book, he is meticulous about accuracy of details.

Born in Riderwood, Maryland, Mr. Frame was raised and educated in various parts of the country. He and his wife and two daughters now live in New York City.

Mr. Frame does fashion and advertising illustration, and he has illustrated over 50 books. Among them are Garrard's *Mississippi Steamboat Days, David Glasgow Farragut: Our First Admiral,* and *The Game of Football.*

Date Due

AG 15 '68	AP 2 '74	APR 26 '78	MAY 14 1983	88.08000		JUL 30 1998
APR 23 '70	DE 11 '74	JUL 31 '78	MAY 1 '84	DEC 23 1987		
OC 13 '70	DE 21 '76	APR 16 '79	MAY 11 '84			
NO 30 '70	JA 19 '77	APR 27 '79	DEC 20 '84	NOV 14 1988		
MAR 29 '71	MAR 31 '77	NOV 18 '81	MAY 11 '85	DEC 21 1989		
MR 10 '72	APR 20 '77	APR 1 '9 1982	MAY '11 '85	FACULTY		
FE 6 '74	MAY 9 '77	MAY 14 1982	DEC 19 '85	10-9-90		
FE 25 '74	AUG 05 '77	MAR 01 1983	MAY 9 '86	APR 18 1993		
MR 25 '74	NOV 21 '77	MAR 29 1983		APR. 06 1994		

PRINTED IN U.S.A.   CAT. NO. 23231